Executive Functioning Workbook for Kids

100 Activities and Strategies for Sharpening Critical Thinking Skills, Self-Discipline, Decision-Making, and Planning

Table of Contents

Introduction Letter to Parents

Dear Parents,

You are your child's first-ever role model. Due to your influence in their life, you have the power to guide them in achieving their full potential and greatness. This workbook is designed to be your partner in this journey, providing you with the roadmap for strengthening your child's executive functioning skills. These include time management, focus, self-control, decision-making, and more. They are the foundation of strengthening your child's mind and decision-making skills.

In this book, you'll discover engaging puzzles, interactive games, and hands-on worksheets to captivate your child's imagination and enhance their cognitive abilities. The aim is to help them confidently navigate their daily tasks and set them up for lifelong success by teaching them the skills they need to contribute to their planning, organization, time management, and problem-solving skills.

When nurturing your child's young mind, you will face unique challenges. However, this workbook will make those challenges much easier to manage. While progress is not instant, remember that every step forward is a triumph. Each time your child faces a hurdle, they build resilience and determination. Make sure to avoid making your child feel inadequate whenever they face a problem. Cheer them on and remind them to believe in themselves.

Also, keep an eye on their progress and celebrate their success. Your positive responses and support are invaluable and will go a long way in helping them become successful adults. Thank you for being a part of your child's journey!

Introduction Letter to Kids

Hey there, you awesome reader!

Are you ready to embark on an incredible journey? This workbook will be your guide to something truly fascinating: Executive Functioning!

Did you know that your brain possesses a unique ability that assists you in making wise decisions, maintaining focus, mastering your time, and accomplishing your big goals? This workbook will be your treasure map, leading you to explore and refine this skill.

Moreover, this workbook goes beyond the ordinary. It's filled with enjoyable puzzles, engaging games, thought-provoking worksheets, and much more. These activities will strengthen your brain and improve your confidence.

Here's a little secret: It's absolutely fine if you don't fully understand everything right away. Everyone starts by learning and practicing, just like you're doing now. Progress takes time, and finding joy in each step is crucial.

Whenever you face difficulties or need encouragement, it's important to remember that your journey is based on being able to stick it out; keep trying! Mistakes are a natural part of learning, and each attempt brings you closer to mastering these skills.

So, let's embark on this journey, make the most of it, and uncover the incredible potential of your mind. Good luck!

Section 1: What Are Executive Functioning Skills?

Your brain is the command center for everything you do each day: focusing, memory recall, time management, wise decision-making, and keeping ahead of the game. These things make up what's known as your *executive functioning capabilities*. Using these abilities in your everyday life allows you to focus your attention and structure your day however you want.

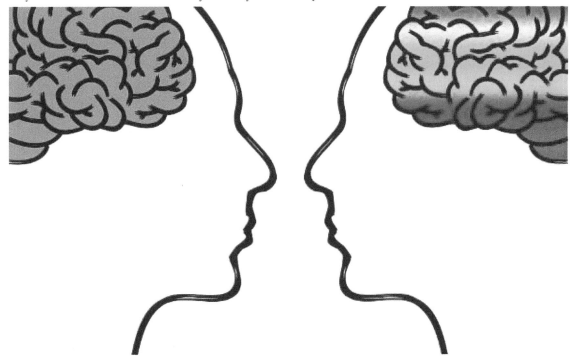

Your brain controls everything you feel and do.

Some kids can struggle to stay focused for a long time or have poor problem-solving, organization, and decision-making skills. When you constantly tell yourself that a certain task is too hard, you actually convince your mind that it is! No matter how hard you try, the situation only gets worse. So, to avoid that, you need to improve your focus, decision-making, and problem-solving skills from a young age.

This section will help you develop your executive functioning skills, such as time management, problem-solving, decision-making, planning and development, self-control, and more. You will find a wide range of exercises to put the things you learn to the test. Remember, your executive functioning skills evolve alongside your personal growth. You can't expect to master them all quickly. Instead, do your best and be patient, and your skills will grow with you!

Components of Executive Functioning That Help You Achieve

Think of executive functioning as what your brain uses to make things go more smoothly. You'll achieve so many things with executive functioning. Those things include:

Cognitive Flexibility

With cognitive flexibility, your brain can easily switch gears. Basically, you can adapt and change your line of thinking when something unexpected happens.

Working Memory

Your brain can act as a notepad. It can remember information like phone numbers and instructions according to how they were given.

Self-Control

This gets you to stop and think before acting on impulse. For example, if you're angry and want to break a plate, your brain will stop you by reminding you of the consequences.

Planning and Organization

Together, planning and organization enable you to plan your life properly. Planning helps you decide what to do and when, while organization helps you arrange your toys or put your shoes on the right feet!

Time Management

Time is difficult to manage sometimes, especially when you have a lot to do. However, you can make the clock your best friend. You do that by learning proper time management and splitting your time between being productive and having fun.

Attention and Focus

Your brain has the ability to focus and pay attention to anything you believe is important enough.

Problem-Solving

With problem-solving, you can figure out your next step when you face challenges in any area of life.

Decision-Making

Whether you're aware of it or not, you make decisions on a daily basis. Decision-making helps you pick the best choice by weighing the good and the bad.

Goal Setting

Goal setting helps you do things safer and better. It helps you decide what to do and how to do it to set your goals.

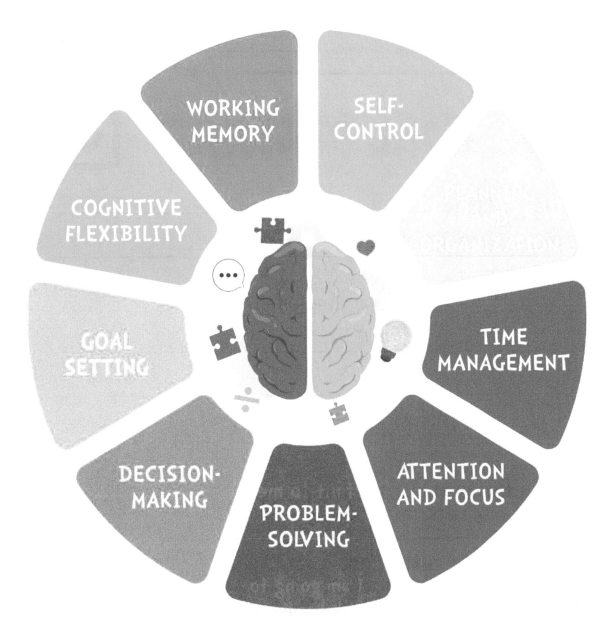

Goal setting helps you align your tasks.

Self-Assessment Skills

With the help of these following activities, you'll learn your strengths in each skill and how you can improve.

1. Setting Your Goals

Set a goal and break it into smaller parts. Give yourself a gold star every time you accomplish one of those parts.

Name: _____ Date: _____

MY GOAL PLANNER ☑

My goal is to: _____
_____

Ways I can work toward my goal:

1. _____

2. _____

3. _____

Why this goal is important to me: _____
_____

New things I will try:	I am going to work harder at:	I will read:
_____	_____	_____
_____	_____	_____
_____	_____	_____

Your goal planner.

2. Practicing Mindfulness

Imagine yourself in a maze, trying to avoid distractions whenever you feel overwhelmed. In your head, with every step forward, take a deep breath.

Imagine yourself in a maze.

3. Decision-Making

It's normal to face tough decisions. All you have to do is take control of your thoughts. Remember, some decisions can be easily avoided. Ask yourself these questions to know if a decision is worth your time.

- Why am I making this choice?
- Would it have a good or a bad impact on me?
- Would it have a good or a bad impact on someone else?
- If not, how can I make it have a good impact?

4. Time Tracking

Time tracking gives you the chance to see how you spend your day. Start by taking a brand new notebook or journal. Make that into your time tracker. At the end of every day, write what you did and how long that took. If you find using a list too boring, use the example below.

Time Tracking

Time tracking helps you arrange your day.

5. Impulse Control

You need to learn to pause and think before taking any action. Try playing games like Simon Says and Jenga to learn to slow down and think before doing anything.

6. Dealing with Procrastination

Learn to deal with procrastination by practicing delayed gratification. This is when you tell yourself you'll get the reward later. Tell yourself that you'll get twice the rewards if you do the task when needed. For every task you don't do, you don't get rewarded.

7. Focus Finders

This exercise involves sharpening your attention skills by finding the difference between two pictures in a set time frame. Time yourself or have your parents do it.

Spot the 8 differences in these two pictures.
*Source: https://commons.wikimedia.org/wiki/File:Spot_the_difference.png: Muband at Japanese Wikipedia, CC BY-SA 3.0
<http://creativecommons.org/licenses/by-sa/3.0/>, via Wikimedia Commons*

8. Empathy Exploration

You can act out other people's emotions to try to be in their shoes. Doing this helps you make decisions based not just on your feelings but *on other people's feelings,* too. When you act out scenarios in your head, you have the chance to understand different emotions.

9. Gratification Garden

Imagine yourself in a garden filled with things you're grateful for. Write them on a petal or draw them out.

Imagine you're in a garden and think of all the things you're grateful for.

Section 2: Strengthening Your Mind

Critical thinking involves imagining and analyzing things and situations to make good judgments. It also involves thinking of the consequences of your actions.

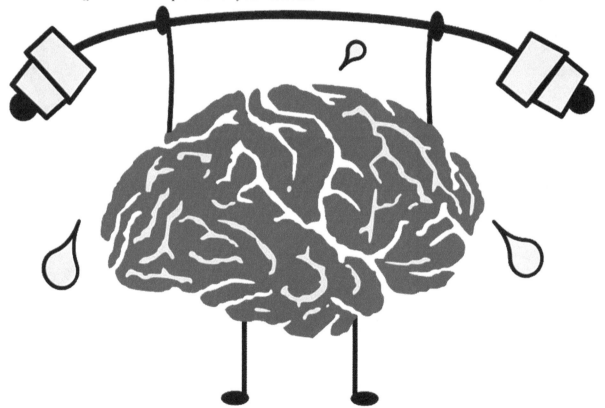

When you use different ways of thinking, your mind gets stronger.
https://creazilla.com/nodes/67261-brain-training-clipart

With critical thinking, you make sound decisions even when no one is there to help you. You choose the right friends, know the best action to take when faced with a problem, know how to avoid troubles for yourself, etc. In this section, you'll be learning additional E.F. skills that can help boost your critical thinking.

Critical Thinking Made Easy

Critical thinking can be a bit complex to understand; here are some helpful tips you should be aware of to help you get started as a critical thinker:

- **Open Mindedness:** With critical thinking, you learn to stay open to new ideas from other people. This would help you understand various viewpoints better.
- **Comparing and Contrasting:** With critical thinking, you learn to compare the different ideas and information that come to you. Understanding the differences and similarities in the things around you helps you see the bigger picture.
- **Inquisitive:** Critical thinking encourages you to ask a number of questions about what you see, hear, and read. For example, "How is this done?" "Why does it happen anyway?"
- **Reflect and Learn:** When you've examined the information before you or have gotten the views of others, you now learn to form your own opinions and conclusions, making well-informed decisions.

Executive Functioning Skills for Critical Thinking

Critical thinking is a skill that builds on the foundation of executive functioning.

Critical thinking skills.

Reasoning

This is the process of thoroughly thinking about something. Reasoning makes you a good problem solver. When you take your time and push your mind to think carefully about things, you develop the ability to solve puzzles and answer tricky questions.

Analyzing

This is like going on an adventure with a magnifying glass. When you analyze things, you get to look at them closely and spot hidden clues. That helps you understand big ideas and tricky problems so you'll be ready to tackle anything that comes your way. For example, a soccer game is not about kicking the ball in any direction you feel like. The aim is to score, so you must find ways to make that possible with so many other players on the field.

Evaluating

This is like having a map to get you to that destination. You'll have to trace the best path by mapping out the good or bad spots and the dead ends. This will help you make smart decisions about friends, games, etc. In the soccer example, you evaluate the possibilities of scoring through your thought-out plans after you've analyzed them. Doing this will make you more careful of your next move.

Metacognition

This is like having a special force that watches over your thinking. You're careful to act because you don't want to make mistakes, so you think through your entire process again. When you use this power, you'll be able to understand yourself better and fix things if they're not going smoothly. If your game plan isn't going as you imagined it, go back to your process and look for where the error began to make corrections.

Decision Making

Being a great decision-maker is like leading a team of players to victory. When you think of things from this perspective, you can hardly make bad decisions because you know that if you do, your choices will negatively affect the people around you. You must steer your choices in the right direction. You must be prepared to pick the best choice, from little choices like what snack to have to big choices about hobbies or goals.

These critical thinking skills are the most important tools you need to have in your toolkit. They will help you solve challenging issues and make awesome choices.

Critical Thinking Worksheet

10. Follow the Clues

Imagine you're searching for a lost toy, just like a detective does. Draw or describe the clues you have on where to find the toy. For example, ask questions like, "When did I last see the toy?" "Who was the toy with?" "Where was the person?" "What possible place could the person go from there?" and anything else you could think of. You can use this method to find anything. Write down more clues you draw out from the toy search examples in the space below.

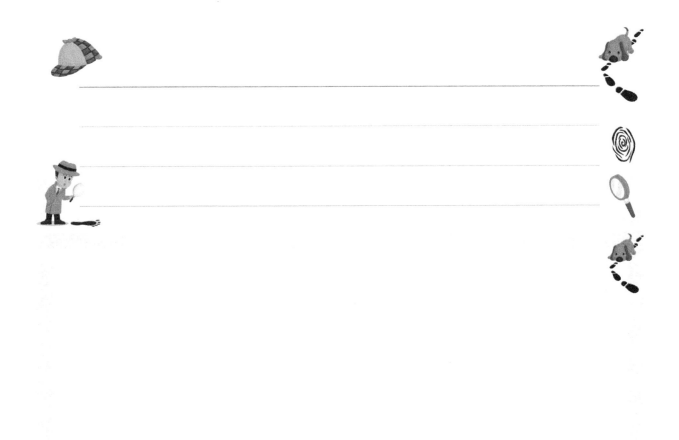

Describe the clues that will help you find the toy.

11. Spot the Differences

This exercise helps you focus on even the littlest details to notice differences in events and situations. Circle the difference in each picture.

Find the 7 differences

Spot the difference.

You can even apply this exercise in real life by looking at two days in a row, say today and yesterday, and seeing what you did differently.

12. Making Tough Choices

Imagine you're on your way to the park with your friend. Suddenly, your friend finds a purse. What will you do, and why will you do it? This exercise teaches you the difference between right and wrong and how the choices you make can affect the lives of others. Write down three different things that can happen in this case, and tick the best option from your list. Also, below each decision, write out how you think the purse's owner would feel about it.

☐ _____

_____

☐ _____

_____

☐ _____

_____

Write down how you think the purse owner will feel.

13. Problem-Solving Adventure

Imagine you're on a camping trip and must use the map below to find your way. Trace the lines in the map to show the safe part to take. This teaches you to solve problems and find creative solutions when faced with roadblocks.

Trace the lines in the map to find your way.

Critical thinking is a very helpful tool in building your brain muscles. It is all about using your willpower to make good decisions. It helps you think long-term about how much your choices will affect you and others. The exercises in this section are meant to help you make real-life choices. It can be fun and exciting when you figure your way out of things and discover answers to tricky questions. This skill takes time to develop, so do different exercises daily to help you stay on track.

Section 3: Training Your Willpower

Similar to how you run and jog to train your legs and body, it's necessary to train your brain muscles to make good decisions and stick to your goals. However, this can only be achieved through self-discipline and willpower. Self-discipline is your brain's ability to say 'no' to things. For instance, when you tell your brain, "Today I'll skip the chocolates so I can save them for a movie," it automatically forces your body to respond to your decision.

On the other hand, willpower is like a mind muscle that helps you stay focused and motivated on what you tell your brain to do. When you've decided to do something, you may not get encouragement from things or people around you, so training your mind to give you all the strength and encouragement needed to keep going despite the odds is where your willpower comes into play.

Get your mind ready to practice fun exercises to help you build your self-discipline and willpower. You will also learn about delayed gratification and how it keeps you excited and enthusiastic about doing anything.

What Is Willpower?

Willpower is an invisible force that pushes you to do the necessary things. For example, doing the dishes, not because you want to but because it's necessary. Your willpower pushes you to do what's needed of you, such as doing your homework, cleaning your room, and so on. The adults around you call it *motivation*, but it's a force, a voice that encourages you to keep climbing and pushing toward what you want. Just as push-ups make the arms grow strong, practicing self-discipline and willpower builds your confidence and strength to carry out any task.

How to Apply Self-Discipline and Willpower

There are many helpful ways to apply self-discipline and willpower skills when needed. Firstly, identify something you think is difficult to carry out, and follow the steps below:

14. Start Small

If you ever want to begin weightlifting, which weight do you start with? Do you go for the ones that are impossible to lift or what you can handle?

Applying self-discipline and willpower should begin with small challenges that are easier to handle. For example, immediately after you get home from school, you could jump right in front of the TV, head out to the kitchen, or pick up your tablet to watch videos. Instead of doing these things, you could put your school things away and have a warm bath first.

15. Make Plans

Making a plan can make you more successful.
https://pixabay.com/vectors/presentation-statistic-boy-1454403/

Plans help you set priorities. Therefore, plan before making certain choices. If you know it's essential to do your homework before playing, stick to your plan by writing down an after-school schedule.

16. Exercise Patience

It is annoying and frustrating to wait for something you desperately want. However, waiting is something you should get used to. The more you practice patience, the stronger your willpower gets.

17. Celebrate Your Wins

Celebrate yourself no matter how little self-discipline and willpower you exercise. Celebrating every win will make you feel happy and proud of yourself.

18. Delayed Gratification

Delayed gratification means that you can wait to get what you want – and practicing this can make a big difference in your life, both now and in the future. It helps you stay patient for something good that's coming along. Your future isn't as far away as you think. After all, it's only a second away! Delayed gratification makes you resist the temptations you feel of having something immediately. In exchange for waiting, you get something better. For example, you're told you'd get one piece of candy before you complete a task, but if you wait until the task is finished, you get three pieces of candy. Which would you prefer? If you chose three, that's a great example of delayed gratification.

My Area of Improvement Worksheet

19. Common Cravings

Make a list of things you often crave, like food, attention, friends, a place, or an object. Be more specific while naming these cravings. You can start with three for now. Think of other possible activities to replace these cravings. Afterward, create a plan on how to do those activities.

An example is drinking water whenever you feel like drinking soda. To do this, you must remove all the sodas around you and replace them with water. Unlike soda, drinking water keeps you healthy by flushing all harmful things in your body.

COMMON CRAVINGS

CRAVINGS	ALTERNATIVE	PLAN

Fill in the common cravings that you have.

20. Distraction Barriers

What are the things that can easily distract you? Write down three on the top of the picture below.

They could be:

- Playing a game when you should be reading
- Watching TV when you should be doing your homework
- Looking at a screen when you should be asleep

Plan a certain task in your free time without being distracted.

What kind of reward would you like to get for focusing?

Write about or draw a picture of the reward you want after focusing in the space to the right.

If you get distracted, put a sticker in the thought bubble space. Your goal is to have less or no stickers with each day that passes.

Draw or write a reward you would enjoy.

21. Procrastination Breakdown

Procrastinating is wrong, but it's a normal feeling. The best way to overcome it is by breaking big tasks into smaller steps. Think of something you've been putting off or avoiding. It could be something you should do but cannot bring yourself to do it. Write what you should do in front of the checkboxes provided for you. Check the checkbox with a colored pen for each goal you complete.

Set a timer for each step and complete them one after the other.

Daily Checklist

Have You:

MORNING:

- [ ] Made your bed?
- [ ] Gotten dressed?
- [ ] Had breakfast?
- [ ] Brushed your hair?
- [ ] Brushed your teeth?
- [ ] Put socks and shoes on?
- [ ] Got your lunch?
- [ ] Got your backpack?

AFTERNOON:

- [ ] Gotten a snack?
- [ ] Done your homework?
- [ ] Read for 20 minutes?
- [ ] Done your chores?
- [ ] Played?

EVENING:

- [ ] Set out clothes and shoes?
- [ ] Packed your backpack?
- [ ] Taken a shower or bath?
- [ ] Put your pajamas on?
- [ ] Put clothes in hamper?
- [ ] Brushed your teeth?

CHORES:

- [ ] _____
- [ ] _____
- [ ] _____
- [ ] _____
- [ ] _____
- [ ] _____

Daily checklist.

22. The SMART Move for Your Goals

SMART is a great way to achieve the plans you set for yourself. Begin by choosing a goal related to your hobbies, school, bad habits, etc. Follow these steps to achieve your goals.

Be Specific (S)

When setting goals, begin with something easily achievable and specific. Do not set goals to impress someone. For example, you could say, "I want to get better at multiplication," instead of, "I'll be better at math."

Be Measurable (M)

Set measurable goals. Write these goals down somewhere so you can easily track your progress. For example, you can track your progress in math by the number of problems you solve easily.

Be Achievable (A)

Set goals that are possible to achieve no matter their difficulty. Avoid aiming too high, but start one step at a time.

Be Relevant (R)

Your goals must mean something to you. If they are irrelevant, how will you achieve them? Therefore, set goals about things you care about improving, or you might lose interest easily.

Be Time -Bound (T)

All of your goals should have a deadline. It is not a goal if no time frame is attached. Set a reasonable time so you can likely achieve your goal.

You'll be one step closer to achieving all your goals with self-discipline and willpower. Engage in each activity in this section to make you into the person you desire.

Section 4: Managing Emotions and Impulses

Managing emotions and impulses is an important part of your overall development. Identifying, expressing, and regulating your emotions improves your emotional, social, and mental health. In this section, you will learn what emotional awareness and impulse control are and why this process is important for avoiding challenging behavior and controlling your emotions. You will also see that emotional and impulsive control are connected to executive functions.

You need to understand all your feelings to control your emotions.
https://freerangestock.com/photos/118921/emotions-expressed-with-black-color-in-yellow-squares.html

What Is Emotional Awareness?

Emotional awareness is when you can understand your feelings and those of others. This is regarded as *emotional intelligence*. Increasing your emotional IQ helps you solve problems by being aware of emotions and regulating not just your emotions but also those of others – for example, cheering your friends up when they are down.

You need emotional awareness to express your emotions to others, like being happy, sad, etc. Only when you become *aware of* your emotions can you manage or control them. You can easily face or avoid tough situations when you develop the power to control your emotions. Being aware of your emotions also teaches you how to set boundaries that work for you and to understand and respect the boundaries of others. When you are emotionally aware, you will say or do things that make you happy and fulfilled. How? You can distinguish between bad and good and choose what feels good over what will make you feel bad.

23. Identify the Emotion

In the table below is a list of emotions. On the other side of the table, give three actions to describe each emotion. This game will help you identify an emotion when you or others play it out.

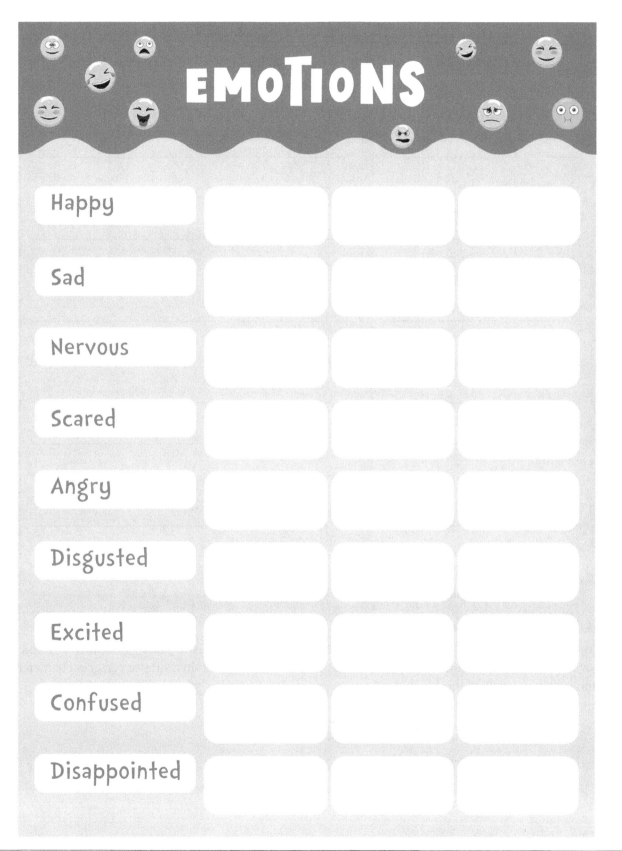

EMOTIONS

Happy			
Sad			
Nervous			
Scared			
Angry			
Disgusted			
Excited			
Confused			
Disappointed			

EMOTIONS	DESCRIBE EMOTIONS
_____	_____
_____	_____
_____	_____
_____	_____
_____	_____
_____	_____
_____	_____
_____	_____
_____	_____
_____	_____
_____	_____

24. Recognizing Emotions

Emotions are physical sensations you feel in your body. Here is a game you can try: Look in a mirror and mimic the "shame" emotion. When you are done doing that, draw a cartoon character that has the look you made in the box below.

Draw a cartoon character with the face you made!

There's no way to describe emotions without a connection to how the body appears or feels. For example, when you are excited or nervous, you feel butterflies in your stomach. That is your body's way of interpreting the different emotions you might be feeling.

It is normal to feel out of control or act on the big emotions you experience at school or home. Nonetheless, the first step to taking control of your emotions is to identify what you are experiencing from your body's cues.

Emotional Control

Emotional control is how you respond to and manage emotional experiences, especially difficult ones at home or school. That includes staying relaxed when nervous, frightened, or excited or remaining calm when disappointed, angry, or frustrated. Emotional control is not doing or saying anything that might cause harm to you or others when experiencing your emotions.

Here are some techniques to learn to control your emotions based on E.F skills:

25. Planning: Make time for chores and to work on class essays or projects.

26. Organization: Arrange how you want to get your work done and what should come before the other. You can use binders with multiple folders to arrange your work.

27. Time Management: You can set alarms to help you know when to round up a task and when to begin another.

28. Using the <u>Stop, Think, and Act</u> technique: In an emotionally intense situation, this technique will teach you to:

- **Stop:** Take a pause or a breath first. You cannot display good emotional control if you act out of control.

- **Think:** Next, identify the problem causing you stress. Figure out a solution or the best way to come out of it.

- **Act:** Go with the best option or plan. Talk to someone if you're not sure of what to do. "I need help" sometimes happens to be the best emotional control.

For instance, someone picked on you in school, which made you so angry that you acted out by getting into a fight. What do you think will be the outcome of that event? You will most likely both be punished, and no one will be willing to hear who is in the wrong.

Now, using the Stop, Think, and Act technique to control your emotions in a situation like this, you can take deep and slow breaths, see how the person's action affects you, and create options to stop them. You can calmly tell the person to stop, walk away, or go to a teacher. Think about the best option for you and go on with your plan.

In the next exercise, your goal is to 'get to green,' which means getting to a calmer emotion that can help you think more clearly.

STOP!

What emotion are you feeling right now?

_____

What does it feel like in your body?

_____

_____

_____

THINK!

What tools can I use to help me get back to green?

_____

_____

_____

ACT!

What tool do I want to use right now?

_____

Did using this tool help me calm down/get to green?

Yes / No

Stop! Think! Act! What do you need to do to get to green?

Never be ashamed to seek help, especially when you don't know what to do. Your parents and the school's counselor are always better positioned to help. A simple call for help could be what you need.

What Is Impulse Control?

Impulse control is the ability to stop and think before you speak, act, or respond. Impulse and emotional control are related. For example, in an intense emotional state like anger, you act aggressively rather than letting the anger dissipate. Their relationship is seen when you react or act quickly without considering the consequences. This is what happens when you hear someone say, 'I acted out of impulse.'

Here are some examples of impulsive behaviors:

Binging: Overdoing things like eating, gambling, or shopping.

Destruction of Properties: Destroy things in moments of anger.

Escalating Problems: When you take something that should not be an issue and make a problem out of it. Your actions in situations like this are termed unnecessary.

Frequent Outburst: Losing your cool for a minute.

Constantly Starting Over: For example, joining a group or club in school today and quitting the next day. Not being true to anything for a long time.

Oversharing: Talking too much without thinking and, in the process, disclosing vital information.

Self-Harm: You hurt yourself in the heat of disappointment, anger, and frustration.

Physical Violence: Getting physically aggressive, e.g., getting in a fight.

Getting Vocal: Yelling or screaming in frustration, especially when you don't get your way.

Interrupting: Forcing yourself in a conversation.

Grabbing: Not willing to wait for a turn, and instead just taking what you want.

Ignoring Danger: Jumping into a pool when you can't swim or running into the streets without looking at the streetlight or if a car is approaching you.

29. How to Manage Your Reactions

Using the chart below, pretend that someone intentionally took your favorite snack from you and threw it away to bully you. Write down three possible reactions to the event in the first column, and from your list, put a check beside any response that represents an *impulsive behavior*. In the middle column, mention the emotion you felt before reacting, and in the third column, write down two potential consequences that an impulsive reaction will cause you.

IMPULSIVE BEHAVIOR	EMOTION	POTENTIAL CONSEQUENCES
_____	_____	_____
_____	_____	_____
_____	_____	_____
_____	_____	_____
_____	_____	_____
_____	_____	_____
_____	_____	_____
_____	_____	_____
_____	_____	_____
_____	_____	_____
_____	_____	_____

How do you react to different behaviors?

Exercises

Here are some exercises to help you minimize impulsive and automatic responses:

30. Guided Breathing: Close your eyes, and then slowly breathe in and out. This exercise will teach you to pay attention to your present environment.

31. Drawing Emotions: Draw your emotions each time you feel them.

32. Yoga and Physical Exercises: All forms of physical exercise can reduce stress hormones and enhance mood and energy levels. Try doing some the next time your emotions feel out of hand.

33. Learning a New Hobby: A new hobby will effectively stimulate your mood and overall well-being.

34. Writing about Your Emotions: Get a notebook to write down your body reactions when you feel any emotion.

35. Mindful Walking: When you feel the weight of emotions, try walking away from that environment. As you do, pay attention to things you can see around you.

When you feel your volcano about to explode...

1. ☐ Take a deep breath
2. ☐ Keep your ideas in your mind
3. ☐ Wait your turn
4. ☐ Let your important ideas out of your mouth

What should you do if you feel like a volcano about to explode?

36. Journaling Experiences: You can write down the events that played out with you and how they made you feel. This would help you be more conscious of yourself and those around you.

what you experienced

how it made you feel

Write down situations where you have felt a certain emotion and how you reacted/felt/dealt with it.

Managing emotions can be challenging. However, by practicing the exercises in this section, you will soon become an expert at regulating your emotions.

Section 5: From Chaos to Order

Do you ever feel like the day is too short? Don't worry! All you need to make the most of your day is the right strategies and skills, like order and structure. This section will equip you with the necessary skills to go about your daily routines without feeling overwhelmed.

Benefits of Having Order and Structure

It's great to feel and stay in charge of your day. To do that, though, you will need to be able to predict your entire day. When your daily routines and activities are planned out, you will perform them better. So, always put some order and structure into place (that means arranging your duties and routines so that moving from one to another becomes easy.) The following are benefits you'll enjoy when you organize your day:

Stress Reduction

You will feel more secure and in control because you know what to expect from your day. If you are uncertain about a particular situation or cannot predict the outcomes based on a lack of structure, you will be stressed due to disorganization and frequent changes.

Efficiency

When you have a clear structure, you will be focused and do better on tasks. You have no reason to fear what to do next because you already know!

Sense of Calm and Control

Having structure and order will help you achieve your goals. You will not be afraid because you understand what to do, and with that confidence, you will face any obstacle to your goal!

Success in School

You can predict how your tests, assignments, and exams will turn out because you follow a well-structured routine. Knowing when to study, rest, or do your assignments will make concentration easier!

Daily Routines and Rituals

Here are some daily routines and rituals to have a successful day:

37. Rise and Shine

When you wake up every morning and take a walk outside for a few minutes, it gives you the feeling that "it is going to be a great day." This feeling improves your mood and energy and lets you go about your day positively.

38. A Good Breakfast

A good breakfast boosts your energy, improves your concentration in school, and helps you to grow. Eating a good breakfast with vital nutrients will help you start your day well.

39. Deep Breathing

Practicing breathing from your belly is good for your health. It helps your body fight against anxiety and is a mood booster for a great day. Spending ten minutes a day doing this exercise will increase your awareness and enable you to remain focused and calm. Before you go to school, take a test, or even start your day, take a few moments to breathe.

40. Take a Walk

Taking a walk can help you clear your mind.

Walking is a very good exercise. Walking barefoot on the grass or the sand on a beach can be wonderful. It clears your mind and supports easy blood flow from your heart to your entire body. Walking in the morning sun exposes you to Vitamin D, a good nutrient for your bones, immune system, and overall well-being.

41. Stretch

Stretching resets your mind and body, especially if you have been sitting for a long time or feeling worn out. Stretching makes you flexible. As you do it, blood and oxygen supply can easily flow to relieve any achy part of your body.

42. Eat Green

Eating veggies is very good for your health.

Having veggies in your diet is very beneficial to your health. No matter how little they seem, they are good for your well-being. Vegetables are a rich source of fiber, minerals, vitamins, and antioxidants. Adding them to meals and snacks helps your day be more positive and productive.

43. Stay Hydrated

Drink a lot of water. Water is good for your skin, mind, and body. When you're dehydrated, you will experience dry skin, feeling sluggish, headaches, and constipation (not being able to do #2 regularly!). These things could get serious for your health.

44. Limit Screen-Time

Spending long hours in front of your phone or computer can lead to depression and anxiety. Learn to limit your screen time before bed. Your phone shouldn't be the first thing you go for when you get out of bed, so keep it out of sight! You can put it in your drawer until you're done with breakfast if you can't keep yourself from scrolling.

45. Sleep

Your day should end with a routine and ritual for sleep. Take a shower, and enjoy every drop of water on your skin. Then, put on your clothes. Make it a habit to sleep and wake up at the same time each day.

Think about your days and develop some routines you can add to the ones above to bring more order to your day. Write them down in the space below:

_____

_____

_____

_____

_____

46. Flexibility

Flexibility enables you to view situations differently and come up with solutions to new problems. Below (44-47) are ways to develop flexibility.

47. A Role Model: Observe your parents or teachers to see how they deal with challenges and come up with solutions to problems. Then, start acting like them when you come up against one. Do what the role models in your life would do if they were in your shoes.

48. Seek Opportunities: Look for ways to practice flexible thinking. Attempt any task or assignment given to you, no matter how difficult.

49. Reward for Flexible Thinking: Look for ways to be complimented or rewarded for problem-solving by thinking flexibly.

50. Offer Alternatives: Regularly offer alternative ways to use, say, and do things. It shows how flexible you are.

Exercises

Here are some exercises for planning and organizing your tasks and responsibilities by order of importance.

51. Plan Your Day Before Going to Bed. The night before, you must prepare whatever you require the next day.

52. Introducing a Checklist. Even if it is a simple "Vacation list" or "two things to do before bed," having one will encourage you to organize and strategize your time.

53. Have a Kid-Friendly Planner. It will show that you value how well you manage your time and activities; ask your parents to find you one or look online to find one.

54. Develop a Homework Routine. You'll get through this after-school job easier if you do it at the same time each day!

- **Cultivate an Interest in Collecting.** Get a collection box if you are interested in a particular thing. It could be picking up rocks and saving them in your box.

- **The Family Calendar.** You can put things you should and want to do in the family calendar. Your exam dates, holidays, school trips, assignments due dates, etc. should be marked on it. That will make you remember important dates.

Daily Planner

Date:

S M T W T F S

SCHEDULE

6 AM	
7 AM	
8 AM	
9 AM	
10 AM	
11 AM	
12 AM	
1 PM	
2 PM	
3 PM	
4 PM	
5 PM	
6 PM	
7 PM	
8 PM	
9 PM	
10 PM	

THINGS TO DO

NOTES

Your daily planner.

Print out the above template and make copies of it to use each day for a week to see how Your days become more orderly and structured. You can plan your daily activities in this template before going to bed or immediately after you wake up in the morning. However, *doing it the previous day is better.*

Structure and organization will help you to feel safe and in control of your environment. You will understand your current moments and easily anticipate what will come after. It gives you room to do your task diligently and stimulates you to learn.

Section 6: Staying on Track

ADHD and ADD (Attention-Deficit/Hyperactivity Disorder and Attention Deficit Disorder) may cause some obstacles, like difficulty in paying attention, losing your focus easily, and feeling uncomfortable being in a place or performing a task for a prolonged time. Not to worry, this section is designed to equip you with effective strategies to help you stay on track, manage your distractions, and enhance your focus.

Inattention and Distractibility

Inattention and distractibility go together. In essence, when someone is inattentive, they tend to get distracted too easily, and this can cause attention deficiency. However, these two terms are not exactly the same. Someone who is inattentive has issues paying attention. They are often described with words like daydreaming, absent-minded, careless, or neglectful. Distractibility, on the other hand, is said to occur when you start concentrating on an activity but easily lose focus along the line. Your attention is easily divided, and these distractions can be caused by external factors or by your thoughts.

What Is ADHD and ADD?

ADHD and ADD are terms that refer to a state where you may find it challenging to sustain your attention or control how you respond to things. You can imagine this as having a brain that works a bit differently, one with a spark of energy and creativity. It's not all bad; having ADHD or ADD means you possess unique strengths and abilities. While focusing on things might require extra effort at times, these conditions are often accompanied by exceptional creativity, problem-solving skills, and boundless enthusiasm. You shouldn't feel odd learning about this, but instead, you should learn to embrace your neurodiversity, which means recognizing and celebrating the diverse ways your brain work. It's about understanding that everyone's mind is wonderfully unique and that by learning strategies to manage your focus and harnessing your strengths, you can confront situations with confidence and scale through.

Common Distractions

Here are some common distractions you may be struggling with:

Objects

When you're hyperactive, it's very likely that you would easily be distracted at that time. You find yourself picking things and playing with them without even noticing. To help yourself in such cases, try using a stress ball to help you manage your distractions.

Itchy Clothing

Sometimes, when some clothes feel itchy to you, you may have a hard time paying attention. It's because every kid's brains work differently with things like sounds, touches, and sights. How the clothes feel on your skin might be something that often distracts you. So, if something like your socks feel super itchy, it can be really hard for you to focus on other stuff. Try wearing clothes that make you feel more comfortable.

Movement

When you struggle with the focus issue, you may find it hard to ignore any slight movement. The best way out of this is to look for a place with less movement and away from the window or traffic. This would help you to manage your focus, whether studying or playing a game.

Your Thoughts

Thoughts can make you wander off, like daydreaming. So, it's helpful to break your tasks into smaller parts so that you can stay focused more easily.

Ways to Calm Yourself

Having all these distractions buzzing in can sometimes get tricky, but you can beat that; you can overcome that, and here are some tips to help out.

55. Secret Hideout: One tested and proven way to get away from most distractions is by finding yourself a secret hideout where you can escape the noise and take some rest. You can make it fun and cozy, fill it up with pillows and a drawing book and also some toys.

56. Music and Dance: It's no news that songs do make the mind feel at ease when stressed. So you can choose to listen, sing, or just dance to the rhythm of your favorite song.

57. Imaginary Adventure: Another creative way to get rid of the distraction is to imagine you're on an adventure exploring a magical and fun city. This would help keep your mind away from the distraction and make you focus. You can try this when you're too busy and want to zone out of those tasks for a minute or two.

Mindfulness Techniques

Meditation can help you become more mindful.

Mindfulness is one way of keeping your attention in the present and maintaining calmness. Here are some helpful techniques:

58. Mindfulness Breathing

This is a simple yet powerful exercise. It is simply figuring out your in-breath and your out-breath patterns. In mindful breathing, the object of your focus is your breath. Each time you breathe, it's a sign that you are alive and, in the present, enjoying every moment. Take a moment right now, and breathe in, count for 5 seconds, then breathe out. You can repeat this exercise until you redirect your focus back to the task on the ground.

59. Concentration

Concentration entails following your breath-in, breath-out exercise from beginning to end. If your breath lasts four seconds, then your mindfulness is to that degree. Following your breath in this way keeps you in the present.

60. Awareness of Your Body

This exercise entails being conscious of your breathing, surroundings, and yourself. Although this simple exercise comes from your breathing, its effects will redirect your focus to what is before you.

Internal and External Distractions

Here are some internal distractions that can affect you:

- Confidence
- Self-esteem
- Thought patterns

Emotions Here are some external distractions that can affect you:
- Weather
- A phone ringing
- Outside noise
- Pedestrians and cars
- Information overload
- Friends

DISTRACTION LOG

DATE		TIME	

TASK AT HAND

CAUSE OF DISTRACTION

DESCRIPTION OF DISTRACTION

DURATION OF DISTRACTION

STRATEGY USED

Your distraction log.

Here are some activities that can help you manage both internal and external forms of distraction.

61. Set Some Time to Meditate: You should find time to meditate for at least ten minutes daily. It will enhance your attention skills.

62. Manage TV Time: Don't spend your whole day watching TV. Get up and engage in more productive activities.

Do more productive activities other than watching TV.
https://www.pexels.com/photo/person-pressing-the-button-of-a-remote-control-5202957/

63. Do Homework at the Same Hour Every Day: That helps you form a good habit.

64. Practice the Pomodoro Technique: The Pomodoro technique breaks down long study hours into chunks with rewards or breaks between each short session. This technique will help reduce distractions and stress to help concentration.

65. Practice Belly Breathing: That helps you handle challenging situations.

66. Play Concentration Games: Games like puzzles and memory games are needed to develop your attention and focus.

67. Use a Fidget: You can fidget around and concentrate/stay on task at the same time!

68. Mind-Body Integration: You simply sit on a chair without being distracted. Stimulate yourself by trying to break your record every time you repeat this exercise.

69. Remove Any Visual Distractions: It is easier to get distracted when things like the phone, television, or other individuals interact before you. Remove unnecessary clutter and any visual experiences from your space.

Dealing with ADHD and ADD can make you a bit different from others based on how you focus and pay attention to things. Over time, you may have been given the wrong label because of how much you've struggled with this constraint. In the course of reading through this chapter, you must have discovered that it was solely crafted with principles and strategies to help you overcome that inability. Mind you, to become a better person, you need to do much more than just surface reading, you'll need to practice and implement each lesson with consistency. The good news is you do not have to do it alone. Allow your parent or guardian to assist you on your journey of transformation.

Section 7: Mastering Your Working Memory

Working memory enables you to remember and process information for activities like organizing, following instructions, paying attention, reading, etc. Some tasks will be difficult, and you could struggle with school activities without a working memory. A working memory contributes to your brain's enhancement. For instance, if you're given a recipe for baking a cake, your working memory allows you to recall the ingredients you need AND the cake-baking steps, too.

Mastering your working memory is a process, but not all that hard! In this section, you'll learn more about your working memory, its advantages, and how to master it through various exercises. You'll also learn about *dual-tasking, multitasking,* and *attention-focusing.*

Working Memory and Its Capacity

Working memory involves holding onto information in your head when learning and doing different things.

It helps you break down tasks and finish them. With a good working memory, you'll find it easier to follow instructions, and everything you do will get done better! Working memory is used in the following ways.

WORKING MEMORY

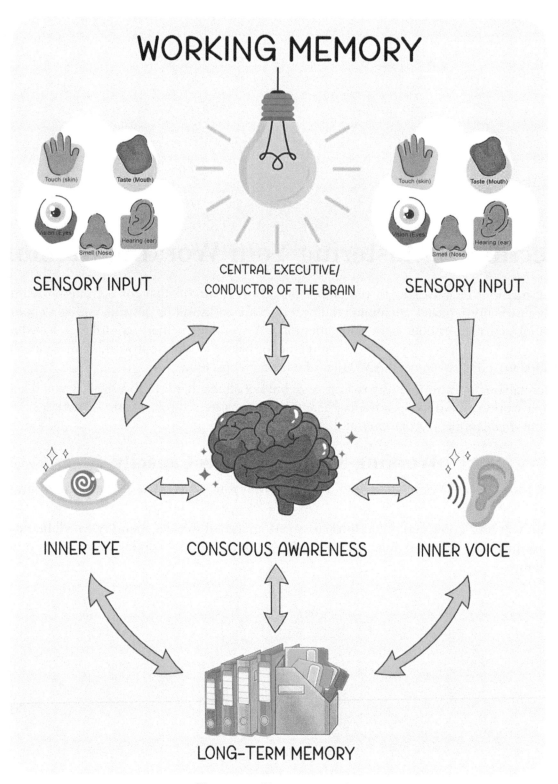

How your working memory works.

How working memory works is that you use your senses to see, feel, smell, taste, or hear something, then you become aware of it.

Your brain then works to understand what those senses do and how they feel. And then stores it in your long-term memory.

Your long-term memory is where you brain keeps information that you can remember and use for a long time when you see, feel, smell, or hear something again.

It can also do these things!

- **Doing Mental Arithmetic** – This is when you do math in your head. When you remember things like 2+2=4, it will help you add up things you see around you.
- **Memorizing Numbers** – Sometimes someone will tell you a number, like their phone number, or the number of times they ate their favorite food.
- **Instructions** – When someone explains steps to do something, like how to make your favorite snack or how to find a classroom at school.

Remember! You can only hold three to four items' worth of information in your mind in one go. For example, "Walk to aisle four, pick up a red shirt, and go to the cashier" will be easier to remember if you're going to the mall for the first time. But if your instructions are "Walk in the door on the right, go to aisle four, say hello to Tom, find a red shirt, find a brown belt, say goodbye to Beth, walk to the cashier and pay, then come back out through the left door," you will probably forget some of that!

Improving working memory means you can pay attention, plan, understand, make decisions, and solve problems.

How Focused Attention Enhances Working Memory

It's normal to be distracted when doing activities or tasks. However, distractions make it more difficult to keep information for a certain period.

While it's normal to have a short attention span, it affects you at home and in school. For instance, you will fail if you're asked to multiply 3 and 5 and don't remember the numbers and steps due to distractions. So, for working memory to *work*, you must practice focused attention.

Focused Attention helps you keep information in your mind. It feeds information to your brain's memory. For instance, if you focus on the information about finding your mom's purse, you'll be able to find the purse easily. If your attention is divided, your working memory will not work right. In class, you should focus more on *what is said* than a bird flying outside the window or a friend sneezing.

Working memory helps you pay attention to whatever information you receive. Not everyone has a working memory, so talk to your parents if you find it hard to stay focused.

Facts You Should Know About Working Memory

Do you know that working memory helps you with schoolwork and other activities? These are other facts you should know about working memory:

- Working memory and attention depend on each other.
- It helps you with learning how to read.
- It helps you with math.
- It also helps you keep and understand whatever you read.
- Through working memory, you'll reach your full potential.

- Working memory also assists you in other activities such as sports, cooking, drawing, etc.

Dual-Tasking and Multitasking

Working memory leads to dual-tasking and multitasking. Dual-tasking and multitasking involve doing two or more tasks simultaneously with focused attention, for example, holding a piece of information in mind while simultaneously doing another thing like recalling or writing. In note-taking, you're either listening to your tutor or reading from the board and writing. When solving a problem, you must recall numbers and the steps involved and solve the problem mentally.

Dual-tasking and multitasking are skills you must possess. If you lack them, your working memory will not come to fruition. Sometimes, doing more than three things or holding more than two information items in mind is difficult. For this reason, the following are tips for managing multitasking:

Pay Attention

The importance of focus in multitasking cannot be said enough! When you're focused, multitasking becomes easier. You stay focused by avoiding distractions and concentrating on specific information.

Know Your Boundaries

While multitasking is necessary, you should know your strengths and weaknesses. If you realize certain tasks are difficult, tell the adults who take care of you.

Prioritize

A great way to deal with multitasking is to prioritize information and tasks. Know which thing to do first, like chores or things your parents ask you to do. If you know you are supposed to clean your room, eat dinner, wash your hands, put on your jammies, and help with the dishes, *some* of those things are done in a specific order, right? Prioritizing is all about doing them in the right order!

Practice

Practice tasks you've done before to retain information.

Exercises and Games to Build Working Memory

70. Active Reading

Active reading can help you absorb information.
https://unsplash.com/photos/man-in-white-crew-neck-t-shirt-and-black-pants-holding-green-plastic-bag-mAWXGoNL0Dc?utm_content=creditShareLink&utm_medium=referral&utm_source=unsplash

Active reading skills assist in absorbing information. Pick any book, underline passages, and discuss what you've read with your parents or friends.

71. Break Down Information

Information is remembered better when broken down into bits. Think of any information. It could be an instruction for a recipe or steps to an arithmetic problem. Break them down into bits and write in these spaces.

_____

_____

_____

_____

72. Is It True?

This game involves jogging your memory through visual and written representation. You must write down if the sentences beneath the picture are true or false. Take time to read each sentence and study the picture.

A little girl riding a bicycle. She is putting on a brown skirt and a blue top.

This woman is holding her baby, the baby is dressed in overalls.

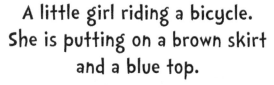

comment if it is true or false

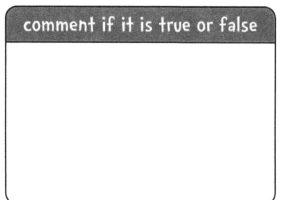

comment if it is true or false

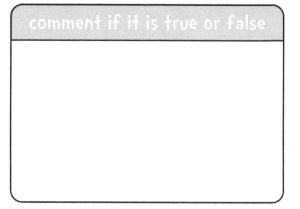

True or false?

73. Visualize

Visualizing scenarios activates your working memory. When you visualize, write down or draw the things you see. Do these exercises:

Visualize a gift you want from a loved one for Christmas. Draw the gift in the space below.

Draw the gift you want!

Also, visualize what a happy day will be for you and write down three ways you will react.

Think about a happy day and write down what you feel when it happens.

74. Memory Game

In the memory game, you'll get to look at images and where they're placed, and then they are placed face down in the same place. You then take have to remember where two matching images are.

It's a challenge to help you see how well you can remember things. Your performance in everything is tied to your working memory.

MEMORY GAME

✂ - - - - - - - - - - - - - - Print twice and cut out the cards -

75. Follow the Path

Learn to navigate through a maze-like puzzle, following a sequence of symbols or colors to find your way out. This is just like being a detective solving a mystery. With the help of this game, you would learn to practice remembering sequences and using them to guide your way through tricky situations.

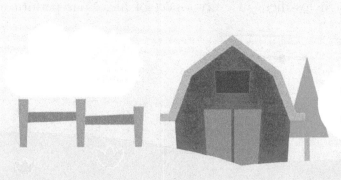

- ● Red means go RIGHT
- ● Blue means go LEFT
- ● Yellow means go UP
- ● Purple means go DOWN

Yellow,
Red,
Yellow,
Blue,
Purple,
Red,
Yellow,
Red,
Purple,
Blue,
Purple,
Blue,
Yellow,
Red,
Yellow,
Red,
Purple,
Red,
Purple,
Red.
Yellow,
Blue,
Yellow,
Blue,
Yellow.

Everyone should have a memory that helps them in every aspect of life. Your performance in everything is tied to your working memory.

Section 8: Decisions, Decisions

Decisions are a big part of your life. You make decisions daily, both consciously and unconsciously. Waking up and choosing to get out of bed instead of sleeping in is a decision. Likewise, choosing to do your homework instead of watching TV is a *conscious decision* (it takes some effort!).

Every decision you make matters, whether big or small. They always have a result, which could be negative or positive. Your decision to do your homework or not will either lead to getting detention in school or getting a reward. As you grow, you should learn how to make decisions. While it's also good to depend on your parents in your growing stage, there are a few decisions you should make for yourself. Decision-making is an executive functioning skill that shapes your mental growth. Good decision-making skills could be difficult, especially with many alternatives. Don't worry, though; you're about to conquer this difficulty.

This section will guide you through the steps of decision-making, the negative and positive consequences of decisions, and relevant factors to bear in mind during your decision-making process.

Why Decision-Making Is Necessary

Decision making skills.

Decision-making is necessary for your growth and development. When you do things on impulse and without going through a process, you don't get the best results! PLAN before making a decision.

Plus, being able to make little decisions, such as the costume you want for Halloween or the snack you want during recess, feels rewarding. You'll feel a sense of pride associated with making decisions on your own.

Builds Confidence

When you make a decision that has a positive outcome, you will feel your confidence level increase. On the other hand, a negative outcome can also give you the confidence to make better decisions about that the next time!

Exposes You to Consequences

With your parents always making decisions for you, it's not easy to realize that not everything works out. Decision-making exposes you to consequences. Through decision-making, you'll learn the effects of choices on you and others. You'll grow when you learn from these consequences.

Encourages Critical Thinking

Decision-making opens different scenarios and possible solutions. This skill encourages critical thinking through asking questions and evaluating options.

Improves Problem-Solving Skills

The whole process of decision-making is about identifying a problem and solving it. Therefore, decision-making improves problem-solving skills in every aspect of your life. For instance, decision-making processes will help answer questions in school and other situations.

Promotes Independence

You're not always going to be around your parents or guardians. Therefore, making decisions at an early stage will promote independence. When you start making your own decisions, you'll grow into a capable adult.

Fosters Resilience

You'll become resilient (can bounce back easier) when you go through negative outcomes from bad decisions. Your mind and soul will be prepared for difficult moments and setbacks. It'll drive you to push forward and become a better person.

Decision-Making Process

Decision-making is a process. It involves identifying a situation, gathering information, evaluating available options, choosing, and acting.

76. Identify the Decision

The first step in decision-making is identifying the decision to make. This process involves asking yourself specific questions such as:

- What is the decision?
- Why should I make this decision?
- Who does this decision affect?
- Is there a deadline?

77. Gather Information

Gather the information needed to make your decision. Take note of other options available for the decision. Ask yourself:

- What are my wants?
- What are my needs?
- What are my principles?

Any information you gather should align with your values, goals, and ethics.

For example, get information on the available action if you're asked to make your bed before a given time. Decide what options go with your principles.

78. Weigh the Pros and Cons

Determining the pros and cons of each decision can help you choose what decision to make.
https://pixabay.com/vectors/decide-decision-choice-choose-vote-6867611/

Since each decision has either negative or positive consequences, weigh these consequences to know which one works best for you. For instance, decide if getting praised for doing the dishes is better than being punished for not doing them.

When you weigh the options for making a decision, you can decide based on which consequence feels good. A decision that feels good aligns with your goals or values. For example, figure out if failing to study for a test *aligns with* (will help you or not) your goal of getting an A grade.

79. Make a Choice

Making a choice comes after weighing the pros and cons of a decision.
https://pixabay.com/illustrations/sign-direction-kids-cute-paint-2792576/

After weighing the pros and cons, it's time to decide. Whatever choice you make should be something you feel good about.

80. Take Action

Once you've made a choice, the next step is to implement it. If you're unsure how to take action, seek help from an older person. Remember to make a plan for your action because it organizes the process.

81. Evaluate the Outcome

You've now taken action. Now, it's time to evaluate the outcome of your action. Ask yourself:

- Did I solve my problem or not?
- Would I choose this decision next time?

Assessing the outcome of your decision will determine if you'll use it again.

Exercises

82. Decision-Making Sheet

Write out the decisions you'll make in the following scenarios. Show your answers to your parents or guardians so they can assess them. Before you answer anyone, carefully consider your options and review your goals and the consequences of your decision.

- 'A friend needs my shirt. I don't need it anymore. What should I do?'
- 'I want candy, but Mom said I must do the dishes first. What should I do?'

Use these steps:

1. Identify the problem.
2. List options for solving the problem.
3. Weigh the pros and cons.

83. Decision-Making Game

Let's play an interesting game. It's a game to test your skills in decision-making, and below are some real-life scenarios where you have to choose the best option that suits you at a time. You'll be given a box to explain why you made those choices. Here we go:

Scenario 1:

Scenario 1: Imagine your family is having a surprise movie night, and you only got to hear about it after your friend had already invited you for a super cool sleepover. Which would you choose, and why would you do that?

Scenario 2: You love art classes, and you also love soccer, but both activities take place after school at the same time! Which would you go for, and why would you do that? Remember that there is no wrong choice in all these. This game helps you understand what is more important to you at a time when compared to others.

Would you choose the sleepover or movie night and why?

84. Decision-Making Rate Yourself Sheet

Reflect on your ability to make decisions on your own. Think about each question or sentence below, and write your thoughts in the box.

What is your decision-making score on a scale of 1-10? Why?

Reflect on a decision you made recently.

How did that decision help you?

85. Weighing My Choices Worksheet

Think of a real-life scenario where you had a problem to solve and a choice to make. Weigh the pros and cons of your choice.

Things about the good and bad things of a situation.

Decision-making could be tough, but remember, you're not alone. Making decisions is like using a roadmap; you need to follow each step to reach your goal.

Section 9: Be a Flexible Thinker

Here's another important part of executive functioning: *cognitive flexibility*. This skill allows you to solve mental, social, and physical problems. The question is, how do you solve these problems? With cognitive flexibility, your problem-solving approach will be better and more effective. You'll think about different ways to deal with challenges instead of feeling defeated. Aside from problem-solving, you'll deal better with uncertainties, changes, and emotions when you think flexibly.

Not having this skill means you miss other possibilities and may have trouble taking on new tasks or getting used to changes. Imagine you want to go to the mall with your friends, and it begins to rain. If you lack flexible thinking, you will insist on going to the mall, which could result in missing out on whatever fun your friends decide on instead. With strong flexibility, you can look at the situation and decide on other fun activities with your friends instead of being sad.

Although cognitive flexibility has a lot of advantages, some kids struggle to learn this skill. This section will guide you toward improving your cognitive flexibility skills through fun activities. Have Fun!

What Is Cognitive Flexibility?

This skill involves carefully assessing a situation or problem from multiple perspectives (different angles or directions) to make better decisions. It lets you think of new information. A *rigid thinker* will find it difficult to switch between options or adjust to changes in plans, but you'll learn to adjust well and switch options to find new ways to solve a problem. *Set shifting* involves letting go of your old ways and embracing new ones to solve your problems.

For example, when you're given a math problem and feel stuck, flexible thinking will enable you to think of other ways to solve the problem. Additionally, it makes it easier to understand and "switch gears." For example, suppose your parents plan a trip to Disneyland, and the plan changes suddenly due to reasons beyond your control. In that case, you'll be open to other alternatives instead of throwing tantrums. Feeling sad about the change is okay, but bouncing back from it is the best way forward.

Why You Should Think Flexibly

Flexible thinking offers many advantages, especially in real-life situations. The following are reasons why you should think flexibly:

Adapt to New Situations

How do you deal with new situations? Do you throw tantrums and avoid communication with everyone for a while? You should know that change is constant, and there are situations you're used to that will change over time. Through flexible thinking, you'll be able to deal with changes you encounter in every aspect of life by letting go of old situations and embracing new ones. For example, be more understanding when your family has to move to a different country for your parents' new job. Instead of angrily resenting the idea, try to understand the reason for the change.

Enhance Problem-Solving Skills

Flexible thinking enhances your problem-solving skills. When you encounter a problem, it helps you use new approaches to solve unfamiliar problems.

Promote Effective Learning

Flexible thinking helps in different areas such as reading, arithmetic, language learning, studying, and writing. It'll be difficult to adjust your approach to solving problems without flexibility. It'll not be easy to improve when you're rigid and refuse to accept corrective feedback from your teachers and parents. Therefore, accept your mistakes and do better next time in the areas corrected.

Develop Creativity

Flexible creativity promotes creative thinking. Creative thinking is a process involving creating unique solutions to problems. It encourages solving problems more creatively. For instance, flexible thinking will enable you to opt for an alternative if you need something and can't find it.

Improve Mental Health

Rigid thinking leads to poor mental health. You will likely become frustrated whenever you see the bad in every unexpected situation. Life is full of setbacks, but how you let these setbacks affect you matters. Flexible thinking reduces anxiety and mental strain. For example, when you visit a store to get your favorite game and realize it's been sold out, you should be open to other options instead of feeling sad.

Develop Healthy Relationships

Flexible thinking builds healthy relationships with strangers, friends, and family. When you're open to sharing, listening, and accepting ideas from your friends, your relationship with them will grow. Through flexible thinking, you'll easily overcome negative feelings of disappointment and anger whenever you encounter problems with your friends.

Shifting Perspective

You need to shift your perspective when you're in a frustrating or annoying situation. Shifting perspective involves letting go of old approaches and trying new approaches. You should realize that there is more than one way of acting or reacting in every situation. Therefore, staying in an approach without any result should be a push to focus on something else. When you shift your perspective, you'll feel better about things.

Be open to considering other people's viewpoints instead of focusing on only yours. For example, when you want to play a game in the snow with your friend, and they tell you they can't play because of the cold, understand their reason instead of being angry.

Flexible thinking helps with shifting perspectives. Through it, you can assess situations and move from your previous opinion.

Ways to Improve Your Cognitive Flexibility Skills

The following are ways to build cognitive flexibility skills:

86. Observe

When faced with a situation, make the following observations:

- How do you feel about it?
- How do you interpret it?
- How well does it work out for you<
- Is there a better way to interpret it?

Carefully examine yourself; be honest and be open about this.

87. Self-Talks

Talk yourself through problems to choose the right solution. When doing this, use positive words instead of negative words. For example, when an approach fails, ask yourself, "What am I missing" instead of concluding with "I'm not good enough." Remember, *there's always a right solution.* Other ways to motivate yourself to improve is with words like;

- 'There must be a way out' instead of 'I'll never work this out.'
- 'I'll keep trying until I get it.' Instead, ' This is hard. I give up.'
- 'Okay, I'm wrong, but I'll get it next time' instead of 'I'm so dumb.'

Put the words in the right box.

Fill each box above with words that fit the headings.

Exercises and Activities for Improving Cognitive Flexibility

88. Flexibility Rating Scale

Rate yourself on the following flexibility skills and circle the ones you can improve. Write down the steps you'll take to improve these skills.

- Thinking of ways to solve a problem

- Ability to move from an old approach to a new one
- Adjusting to new situations
- Shifting perspectives

Write down the steps that will make these skills better.

89. Storytelling (The Switch)

Storytelling helps you think outside the box. Take a familiar story, like Cinderella, and think of a different ending. Write down or draw a comic to illustrate the ending.

Think of your favorite story and give it a different ending.

90. Find New Uses for Items

Pick up any item around you, and think of three other things for which the item can be used.

91. Scavenger Hunt

Get items like toys, pens, erasers, small toys, or anything you need for a scavenger hunt. Get a friend or family member to place them in different places. Ask for pointers to find these items, then try to locate them. Write down how long it took to find them.

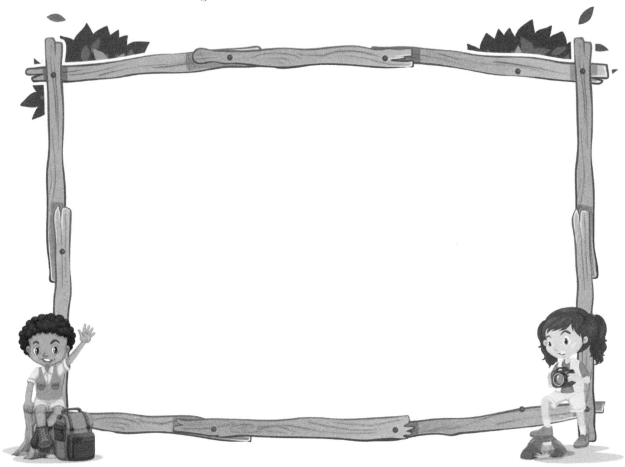

Write down how long it took to find each item.

92. Maze

Find the way out of the maze below.

Find your way to the spaceship.

WORD SEARCH PUZZLE

Find objects in the puzzle and discover the hidden word

CASTLE
KING
QUEEN
PRINCESS
KNIGHT
CARRIAGE
CROWN
PRINCE
BUFFOON

C	A	S	T	L	E	F	B
Q	K	N	I	P	R	I	U
U	C	A	G	C	I	N	F
E	A	K	H	R	R	C	F
E	R	I	T	O	W	E	O
N	R	N	G	Y	N	S	O
T	I	A	G	E	A	S	N
P	R	I	N	C	E	L	E

Find the hidden words.

94. Recreate Drawings

Recreate this drawing.

Draw the cat!

The world is changing rapidly, and there are always new approaches to situations. You need to come up with these approaches yourself. This is why flexible thinking is such an important and needed skill to have!

Section 10: Time Well Spent

Time management keeps you going when you have too many goals and duties. You need this tool to grow up as a successful adult. Some tasks can seem boring or too big for you, so you keep postponing them, even when necessary, such as tidying your room or doing your homework. You only end up piling up things and getting overwhelmed when you postpone your tasks. You don't ever want that to happen. In this section, you'll learn of the many ways to activate time management and how to break very big tasks into smaller chunks to avoid procrastination (which means putting something off over and over again!)

What Is Time Management?

It's important to spend your time wisely.
https://unsplash.com/photos/UAvYasdkzq8?utm_source=unsplash&utm_medium=referral&utm_content=creditShareLink

Time management is simply doing the right thing at the right time without getting distracted. When you know how to manage your time, you will better prioritize your tasks. Time management helps you plan your day, keeping you active and ahead of everyone else.

What Are the Benefits of Time Management?

Here's a list of the many benefits of time management:

- It teaches you how to use your time wisely
- It keeps you ahead of your duties
- It helps you stay organized
- It is a great way to reduce your stress levels
- It teaches you to be responsible
- It sparks creativity
- It teaches you self-discipline
- It helps you prioritize some work over others
- It helps you overcome procrastination
- It teaches you to always be on time and reliable

Breaking Your Goals into Smaller Chunks

Time management can be used to achieve your daily or weekly goals. When you plan to improve in math before the end of your grade year, assuming that's just two months away, you could call this your 'Math Plan.' You need to break the plan into smaller chunks to achieve this. How do you do that? Well, you will have to:

95. Make a Plan

Making a plan means figuring out what you need to do and when you need to do it. It's like mapping out your day to make sure you stay on track and get things done. To create an effective plan, you need to be intentional in areas where you seem to be lagging. For example, it could be studying at the right time, doing your chores without being asked to, or playing only after you've done those important tasks. A plan would simply help you to be more responsible about how you spend your time. You can make good use of this daily planner provided below. Set a time limit to your daily activities. For example, when you return from school at a certain time, you can plan to do your homework and then shower, have lunch, do your dishes and then play a game.

MONTH:

MONDAY	TUESDAY	WEDNESDAY	THURSDAY	FRIDAY	SATURDAY	SUNDAY

TO DO

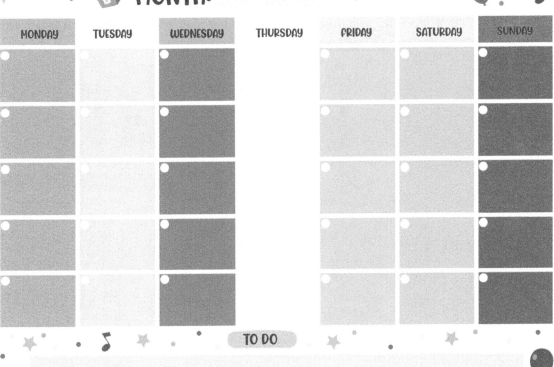

NOTE

EVENT

96. Set a Deadline

Setting a deadline means deciding when you want to finish something. It's like giving yourself a race to see if you can finish before time runs out. To be more practical, you add a time tag to each of those plans you wrote earlier.

97. Create a Timeline for Tracking Your Progress

You can also create a timeline, which is like making a big map of your journey through time. You can mark down important events or tasks and see how far you've come.

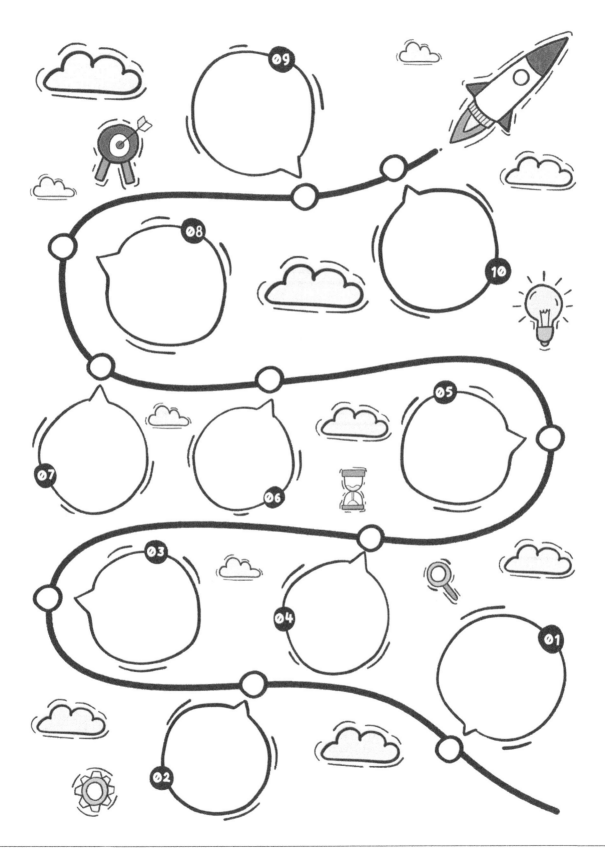

What you've just done is planning. You have a desire in your heart to improve and achieve your vision within two months. That's setting a deadline. In that period, you'd have to create goals. One goal might be to find a study partner. Another goal would be taking extra hours after class to learn new topics. When all these are in place, you can track your progress by looking for how many topics you can cover within a period. It's that easy. Refer to the pyramid below anytime you want to plan your day, tasks, or goals.

create
a plan

set a
deadline

create timelines

How to play your day.

How to Identify Your Priorities

Priorities are just simply placing one task over another. For example, you can either play games or tidy your room. At a certain time, one is good but not necessary for that moment, while the other is not so interesting but necessary for you to do at that time. Here are ways to identify your priorities and set goals to guide you.

98. Write Them Down

Create a checklist for your goals and tick them off whenever you achieve them. How do you do that? You'll need a sticker note or a small notepad. Write on the header "To-Do-List," then write your goals in one section. Then, in another, write down various things or tasks you need to accomplish each goal, from the most to the least important. Form a box at the back of each task so there's room for you to tick them off when you accomplish them. You can use the example below to create yours.

MY GOALS!

- Accomplished!
- Still improving.

- Accomplished!
- Still improving.

- Accomplished!
- Still improving.

- Accomplished!
- Still improving.

Your goals!

99. Important vs. Urgent

This is a tricky but interesting step. You could be stuck in a situation where two tasks need your attention, but if you check well, you will find that one is urgent while the other is important. In this case, focus on the urgent one first. For example, suppose you have a deadline to turn in homework the following day. Then, even if you have important tasks, you should focus on the deadline first.

You should arrange the urgent, important, and less important tasks on your to-do list. Make sure to follow through with your schedule and do one task at a time. There's no need to burden yourself by doing two at a time.

Procrastination

Procrastination is simply willingly postponing any task you have to do without any real or good reason. If you allow it, it will be a big setback for your goals. Here are the causes of procrastination:

- You procrastinate because you're bored
- You lack willpower and self-discipline
- You're afraid to carry out the task
- You manage your time poorly
- You're stressed and too tired to do it

Strategies to Overcome Procrastination

Here are ways to overcome procrastination:

The best way to beat procrastination is to make that large goal look small by breaking it into little tasks. Break them up into smaller parts you can achieve in under three minutes daily? That is much better than taking it out all at once.

Your body only follows what your mind believes, so you can trick it into believing that a task is important to enable you to accomplish your goal.

Another way is through self-talk. You can positively talk yourself into achieving your goals. You should also train your willpower and self-discipline. This has already been covered in section three. You can go back to refresh your memory.

100. Pomodoro Exercise

In this exercise, you will learn to focus your mind and attention on your tasks by using a 25-minute work and 5-10-minute break strategy. You can choose to increase or decrease the work time, and this depends on your capacity. You need a stopwatch or a time tracker and your to-do list for this exercise.

1. Find a quiet spot (not a lot of people around).
2. Turn off all distractions (Games, TV, phones, computers, etc.).
3. Set your timer to 25 minutes.
4. Focus on the activity; if your mind wanders, bring it back to that activity.
5. When the timer rings, take a five-minute break (stretch, talk, drink water, etc.)

You can use this for your studying or when you need to complete any task that lasts more than 30 minutes.

POMODORO TRACKER

Task	#	Pomodoros	DONE
	....	○○○○○○○○	☐
	....	○○○○○○○○	☐
	....	○○○○○○○○	☐
	....	○○○○○○○○	☐
	....	○○○○○○○○	☐
	....	○○○○○○○○	☐
	....	○○○○○○○○	☐
	....	○○○○○○○○	☐
	....	○○○○○○○○	☐
	....	○○○○○○○○	☐
	....	○○○○○○○○	☐
	....	○○○○○○○○	☐
	....	○○○○○○○○	☐
	....	○○○○○○○○	☐
	....	○○○○○○○○	☐
	....	○○○○○○○○	☐

Your pomodoro tracker.

Time management is a must-have skill for everyone. It helps you achieve any goal you've set out to do. Remember these tips:

- You can break your goals into smaller parts and set time frames for each.
- Use your check notes and check off or draw a line across any goal you just achieved.
- Don't let procrastination set in by skipping through your plans.
- You can do anything you put your mind to when you believe in yourself!

A Letter to My Future Self

You should be proud of yourself! Look at how far you've come! Now, you'll write a letter expressing your goals and emotions to your future self. Be as honest as possible because you want to look back and be proud of yourself. This letter aims to keep you on the right path and committed to your goal.

Your letter should include what you hope to achieve. When you're finished writing, lock it in a box. If you feel stuck, don't be reluctant to ask for help from your parents or guardians.

Start by mentioning your age and grade.

Dear (name)

I am _____ years old, and I am in _____ grade.

Follow these prompts for ideas on what to write:

- What have you learned so far?
- How do you plan on putting what you've learned into practice?
- What's stopping you from practicing all you've learned right now?
- What are your goals for this year?
- How and when will you reach your goals?
- What are you looking forward to seeing in the future?
- What advice would you give to your future self?

Thank You Message

Dear Even-more-awesome Reader,

Congratulations on completing this part of your executive functioning journey! It's been a long one, but you've shown resilience and should be proud of yourself. Your dedication and commitment to exploring executive functioning skills are truly inspiring.

Improving your executive functioning skills is a big deal; you've come a long way and should be proud of what you've achieved.

Remember, this journey doesn't have an endpoint. Just like a river keeps flowing, personal growth and learning are ongoing. Keep an open mind and be ready to keep learning new things.

In the materials you've been using here, you've done lots of exercises and activities to help you get better at executive functioning. Keep doing these exercises regularly. Doing things consistently is an important part of this journey, and you'll get even better over time.

Also, don't forget that the real test is using these skills in your everyday life. Take what you've learned and apply it to real situations. That's where you'll see the most significant changes, and I'm confident you'll do great.

Good job for starting this journey and for all the hard work you've put in. Your dedication not only helps you but also makes a positive impact on those around you. You're an example of what can be achieved when you keep trying to improve.

As you continue on this path, remember that your potential is limitless. Your journey shows your determination, and you'll certainly keep achieving great things!

Check out another book in the series

References

10 Effective Emotional Regulation Activities for Kids. (n.d.). Carepatron.com. https://www.carepatron.com/blog/10-effective-emotional-regulation-activities-for-kids

10 Emotional Regulation Activities for Kids. (2022, May 3). Your Therapy Source. https://www.yourtherapysource.com/blog1/2022/05/03/10-emotional-regulation-activities-for-kids/

10 Emotional Regulation Activities for Kids. (2022, May 3). Your Therapy Source. https://www.yourtherapysource.com/blog1/2022/05/03/10-emotional-regulation-activities-for-kids/

5 Fun Ways to Help Develop Your Child's Planning Skills. (n.d.). Foothillsacademy.org. https://www.foothillsacademy.org/community/articles/5-fun-ways-to-help-develop-your-childs-planning-skills

5 Ways to Develop Your Child's Organizational Skills. (2023, March 15). Scholastic.com; Scholastic Parents. https://www.scholastic.com/parents/family-life/social-emotional-learning/social-skills-for-kids/12-ways-to-develop-your-childs-organizational-skills.html

8 Easy Ways to Help Your Child from Getting Distracted. (2022, May 24). The Times of India. https://m.timesofindia.com/spotlight/8-easy-ways-to-help-your-child-from-getting-distracted/articleshow/91638893.cms

Apte, M. M. S. (n.d.). Working Memory in Children: Why It Is Important. Globalindianschool.org. https://blog.globalindianschool.org/working-memory-in-children-why-it-is-important

Executive Functions. (n.d.). Bangkokhospital.com. https://www.bangkokhospital.com/en/content/executive-functions-develop-childrens-concentratio

Beck, C. (2019, January 22). What is impulse control? The OT Toolbox. https://www.theottoolbox.com/what-is-impulse-control/

Beck, C. (2020, June 15). Critical thinking skills. The O.T. Toolbox. https://www.theottoolbox.com/critical-thinking/

Beck, C. (2021, July 8). Emotional regulation and executive function. The OT Toolbox. https://www.theottoolbox.com/emotional-regulation-and-executive-function/

Chambers, Y. (2018, April 27). The best guide for teaching kids the decision-making process steps. Kiddie Matters. https://www.kiddiematters.com/problem-solving-activity-free-printable/

Cognitive Flexibility in Children. (2022, June 30). Cadey. https://cadey.co/articles/cognitive-flexibility

Cognitive flexibility: What is it & why does it matter? (2021, December 29). Braintrust. https://braintrusttutors.com/what-is-cognitive-flexibility/

Darcy, A. M. (2016, May 5). Emotional awareness - what it is and why you need it. Harley TherapyTM Blog; Harley Therapy - Psychotherapy & Counselling. https://www.harleytherapy.co.uk/counselling/emotional-awareness.htm

Dominguez, L. F. (2022, July 24). 7 activities to improve your child's attention and concentration. Homeschool Spanish Academy. https://www.spanish.academy/blog/7-activities-to-improve-your-childs-attention-and-concentration/

Emotional control. (n.d.). Top Doctors. https://www.topdoctors.co.uk/medical-dictionary/emotional-control

Evitt, M. F. (2006, March 30). 7 tips for teaching kids how to set goals (and reach them!). Parents. https://www.parents.com/parenting/better-parenting/style/how-to-teach-kids-perseverance-goal-setting/

Flatley, K., & Certified Parent Educator. (2019, August 29). The trick to teaching kids to manage their own time and get things done (without nagging). Self-Sufficient Kids. https://selfsufficientkids.com/time-management-for-kids/

Flexible thinking. (n.d.). Sociallyskilledkids.com. https://www.sociallyskilledkids.com/flexible-thinking

Gill, A. (2023, March 21). 15 best problem-solving activities for kids to encourage critical thinking. SplashLearn Blog – Educational Resources for Parents, Teachers & Kids; SplashLearn. https://www.splashlearn.com/blog/problem-solving-activities-for-kids/

Hoshaw, C. (2022, March 29). What is Mindfulness: Benefits, How to Practice, and More. Healthline. https://www.healthline.com/health/mind-body/what-is-mindfulness

How to focus a wandering mind. (n.d.). Greater Good. https://greatergood.berkeley.edu/article/item/how_to_focus_a_wandering_mind

Howley-Rouse, A. (2022a, June 17). Developing the components of executive function in the primary school classroom. THE EDUCATION HUB. https://theeducationhub.org.nz/developing-the-components-of-executive-function-in-the-primary-school-classroom/

Jenn Osen-Foss, M. A. T. (2019, October 16). Distractibility. Understood. https://www.understood.org/en/articles/difference-between-inattention-and-distractibility

Leyba, M. (2022, June 10). 20 impactful decision-making activities for middle school. Teaching Expertise; dontan. https://www.teachingexpertise.com/classroom-ideas/decision-making-activities-for-middle-school/

Li, P. (2021, September 27). Critical thinking for kids - 5 powerful ways to teach how to think, not what to think. Parenting For Brain. https://www.parentingforbrain.com/critical-thinking-for-kids/

Morin, A. (2019, August 5). 5 common distractions for kids who struggle with focus. Understood. https://www.understood.org/en/articles/5-common-distractions-for-kids-with-focus-issues

Morin, A. (2019, August 5). Kids use flexible thinking to learn. Understood. https://www.understood.org/en/articles/6-ways-kids-use-flexible-thinking-to-learn

Morin, A. (2019, August 5). Why is working memory important? Understood. https://www.understood.org/en/articles/5-ways-kids-use-working-memory-to-learn

Munir, M. S. (n.d.). Tips to manage distractions in children. Globalindianschool.org. https://blog.globalindianschool.org/tips-to-manage-distractions-in-children

No title. (n.d.). Study.com. https://study.com/learn/lesson/delayed-gratification.html

No title. (n.d.). Study.com. https://study.com/learn/lesson/what-is-working-memory-components-examples.html

Pedersen, T. (2016, January 21). Can you physically feel emotions? Psych Central. https://psychcentral.com/blog/emotions-are-physical

Pietrangelo, A. (2020, May 12). Impulsive behavior: Symptoms, causes, and treatment. Healthline. https://www.healthline.com/health/mental-health/impulsive-behavior

Remez, S. (2020, September 25). 10 tips to increase a child's concentration. Success Consciousness | Positive Thinking - Personal Development. https://www.successconsciousness.com/blog/concentration-mind-power/increase-child-concentration/

Russo, A., & Lf-Apa, W. D. M. (2017, December 8). ADD vs. ADHD symptoms: 3 types of attention deficit disorder. ADDitude. https://www.additudemag.com/add-adhd-symptoms-difference/

San Diego Family Webmaster. (n.d.). Tips to teach kids time management. Sandiegofamily.com. https://www.sandiegofamily.com/parenting/10-tips-to-teach-your-kids-time-management

Schmitz, T. (2016, June 3). The importance of emotional awareness in communication. The Conover Company. https://www.conovercompany.com/the-importance-of-emotional-awareness-in-communication/

Successful goal setting for kids. (n.d.). PlanetSpark. https://www.planetspark.in/blogs/successful-goal-setting-for-kids

The importance of critical thinking for young children - Child & Family Development. (2016, May 3). Child & Family Development. https://www.canr.msu.edu/news/the_importance_of_critical_thinking_for_young_children

Therapy, s. C. (2020, December 16). Why structure and consistency are important for kids. Kids Creek Therapy. https://www.kidscreektherapy.com/why-structure-and-consistency-are-important-for-kids/

Ways to increase your child's attention span. (n.d.). Tutor Doctor. https://www.tutordoctor.co.uk/blog/2022/june/ways-to-increase-your-childs-attention-span/

Wernham, S., & Lloyd, S. (2022, January 22). How to introduce the Pomodoro technique to children. Roxanamurariu.com. https://www.roxanamurariu.com/how-to-introduce-the-pomodoro-technique-to-children

Made in United States
Orlando, FL
20 September 2024

51745301R00059